Milo- The Clean Air Marshal

Ritika Saxena & Dr Pratima Singh

ISBN 979-8-89026-747-4

STEP
CENTER FOR STUDY OF SCIENCE, TECHNOLOGY & POLICY
CAPS

About CSTEP and CAPS

The Center for Study of Science, Technology and Policy (CSTEP) is a not-for-profit policy-research organisation with a mission to augment policymaking through innovative scientific and technological approaches, aiming for a sustainable, secure, and inclusive society.

The Centre for Air Pollution Studies (CAPS) is one of the few entities in India taking an integrated approach to tackling air pollution. The Centre focuses on air pollution studies through measurement, monitoring, modelling, and analysis and engages with relevant stakeholders, including policymakers, to facilitate evidence-based policymaking.

Milo - The Clean Air Marshal

This book belongs to ____________________________

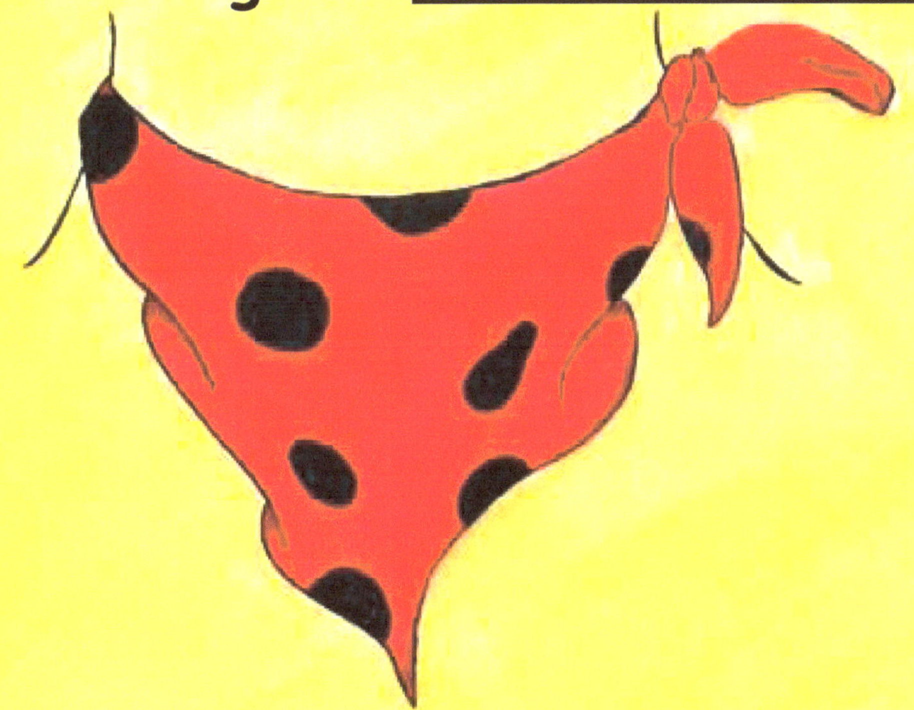

Concept and script - Ritika Saxena & Dr Pratima Singh
Illustrator- Ritika Saxena
Editor- Shayantani Chatterjee

Milo - The Clean Air Marshal

Like any other beautiful, bright day, the morning began with Milo—the naughty, playful, and mischievous dog—chasing a little birdie in the garden.

Rohan, a cheerful little boy, cherished Milo like family. His day would start with Milo and end with him around. They shared a bond that could not be broken. Sometimes they would dress alike with a bandana around their necks. Rohan would treat Milo as his brother. Rohan's parents, Mona and Sahil, were proud dog parents who had a very strong bond with Milo.

Rohan, Sahil, and Mona would play ball with Milo in their beautiful garden every Sunday. This became a family routine on weekends to make Milo feel special. During weekdays, they could hardly get time from their busy lives to pamper Milo and spend time with him.

They lived outside the hustle-bustle of the city, not by choice but due to Rohan's health. Rohan had asthma, and because of the polluted city air, it was difficult for him to breathe properly. So, they moved to the cleaner suburbs a few years ago.

At the end of every month, the family would take Milo out for a picnic at a park. Finally, that day arrived! Everyone was excited for a fun-filled day with food and lots of activities!

Apart from spending a playful day at the park, Milo's favourite moment was to hop onto the back seat of the car and stick his face outside the window to feel the air.

But his happiness was short-lived, as Rohan started feeling uneasy due to the dusty air and started coughing.

Soon, the family reached the biggest and most beautiful park in the city. But, to everyone's surprise, there was a fair at the park and it was too crowded. Cars were lined up way beyond what Milo could see. He was surprised to see such a huge crowd around him.

Sahil dropped Mona, Rohan, and Milo near the gate and went to find a parking spot. While moving inside the park, Rohan spotted someone selling his favourite bear-shaped balloons. He could not wait to buy the balloon and pulled Mona to the balloon stall. Mona lost her hold on Milo's leash. Milo knew what to do. He followed Rohan and Mona.

Suddenly, a crowd rushed in. Milo lost his way and started running in the opposite direction. Milo, being a smart and intelligent dog, remembered that Rohan got excited seeing balloons, so he went after the balloons he had spotted. To his disappointment, it was some other kid holding a balloon and not Rohan. Milo felt LOST.

For the first time in his life, Milo was afraid and didn't know what to do.

Lost and worried, Milo managed to escape the crowd, trying to look for Sahil and their car in the parking lot. Before he could find anyone, a group of street dogs saw him wandering. The dogs started growling and barking at him.

Milo just wanted to reach a safe place, so he started running away from the dogs. The street dogs started chasing him. The more he ran, the farther he was getting away from Mona, Sahil, and Rohan.

Milo finally got away using a shortcut through a slope leading to the other side of the park. This area looked very different. It had small shops, mud huts, and dusty roads, something that Milo had never seen before. Scared and worried about where he was, Milo started panicking, as he was unable to recognize things around him.

He started walking slowly through the narrow and dirty lanes, with people in worn-out clothes. People around him were also surprised to see such a well-groomed dog in their area. Milo kept searching for familiar faces but could not find any. He felt sad and lonely.

Just then, a three-wheeler auto-rickshaw passed by spewing a lot of smoke and roadside dust. Milo's sensitive nose could not handle the smoke and dust, and he started pawing his nose to avoid the pollution.

Exhausted and feeling lost, Milo sat near a lamp post. But he kept changing his position whenever a vehicle passed by to avoid the clouds of smoke and dust around him.

It was getting dark, and Milo was hungry. He was missing his favorite food but was drawn to the food smells from nearby stalls. A thelawala named Mohanlal noticed Milo. Mohanlal looked different from others, as he had a blue bandana tied on his head. He was known for his generosity, and kindness.

He felt sorry about Milo's state and reached out to him. Milo could not resist his humanly care. Wagging his tail, with perked ears, sniffing, and whining, Milo went and sat near him. To Milo's surprise, Mohanlal offered some chapatti and allu sabzi, which his wife had prepared for him. Milo started eating the food happily while Mohanlal caressed him gently. Milo trusted Mohanlal and felt less anxious.

Mohanlal soon realized that Milo belonged to a rich family and did not belong in their area. Mohanlal kept an eye on Milo while selling his food items. Milo, on the other hand, was sad and restless, missing Rohan. Milo would occasionally look around hoping Rohan would find him, but disheartened, he whined and quietly rested his head on his paws.

As the night grew darker, Milo started getting impatient as no one had come to get him. Nobody could have imagined that Milo would come this far away. Mohanlal closed his thela and started preparing to go home. But he was worried that Milo would be alone and the street dogs might bother him. Seeing Mohanlal pack his belongings, Milo stood up and started wagging his tail, as if seeking help.

Mohanlal decided to take Milo to his house. On reaching home, Milo met Bittu, Mohanlal's son, who was of the same age as Rohan. Bittu was a good kid who found happiness in small things and enjoyed every moment. He had lived a challenging life, devoid of basic amenities that kids loved—toys, good clothes, and even access to school. But he never complained about this to his parents. He understood the challenges they faced and was grateful for all their love and care.

Bittu was excited to see Milo and enquired about him. Mohanlal explained to Bittu, 'This dog seemed lost, and we should help him till his owners find him.' Happy to have met a dog, Bittu felt excited and so did Sushila, Mohanlal's wife. Sushila was happy to see that for some time, Bittu will have someone to play with. She smiled at Milo as she started cooking food for dinner.

But, to Milo's shock, she wasn't using a gas stove. Instead, she was using a chulha that used wood and produced a lot of smoke. He remembered Mona preparing food on a gas stove that did not produce any smoke.

Milo wondered, Mona would never use this wood chulha, as Rohan would not stop coughing. Rightfully so, Bittu, Mohanlal, and Sushila kept coughing while the food was being cooked.

Milo pondered why Bittu was so lean and weak. Bittu's poor health was because they were unable to make ends meet. Mohanlal barely earned enough to provide for his family. Bittu had experienced breathing issues for a few years. Due to the lack of proper health facilities in their area, Mohanlal used to take Bittu to a far-away clinic. With treatment and medication, Bittu would be fine for a few days but the condition would resurface again. Recently, his coughing had worsened due to the smoke from cooking and dust from the roads.

Bittu was eager to play with Milo. This cheered up Milo, but it reminded him of Rohan. He sat down in a corner, while Sushila continued cooking in the dim bulb light, hanging from the roof of their hut. Milo looked around and noticed how everything was different from his villa-like home. Though Milo found a loving family of three, their way of living was opposite to what he had seen all his life. The hut had unpainted brick walls, the roof was made of tin and was broken, and there was so much smoke inside the house.

Milo ate chapatti for dinner and chose a corner of the hut, beside Bittu, to sleep.

At dawn, Milo woke up hearing sweeping noises. Sushila was cleaning the hut with a broom. She collected the household garbage in a plastic bag and went outside. Curious, Milo followed her. He saw a tempo standing, making loud noises, and spewing black smoke. Hefelt relieved that Bittu was sleeping inside or else he would start coughing. Milo saw Sushila dump the plastic bag in the tempo. He saw other people doing the same.

Milo got confused, as he remembered that Mona would segregate their garbage into two bins and one bag: one green bin for wet waste, which was usually stinky and full of vegetable peels; one red bin for rejected waste having small pieces of glass or used bandages; one bag for dry waste, in which they would throw chocolate and chips wrappers among other things. Rohan and Milo would play a fun game to put the right waste in the right bin or bag. So, Milo wondered why these people collected all their garbage in a single plastic bag, as this didn't seem fun.

After a while, Mohanlal left for work, and Bittu and Milo followed him. On the way, Milo saw other vendors sweeping their respective areas, collecting their garbage, and burning it. Milo was scared on seeing the open fire. He understood that in this locality some garbage thrown on the road is burnt in the morning after cleaning.

It was time for Mohanlal to prepare his poori-sabji, which was loved by many in the area. As soon as Mohanlal started frying the pooris, a boy visited his shop to buy the food he was selling. As the boy finished eating, despite seeing a dustbin nearby, he threw the paper plate and plastic bowl on the ground. Seeing this, Milo started barking in anger as he remembered the burning waste he saw in the morning.

The boy was startled by the loud bark. Milo started growling at the boy, so he picked up the waste and dropped it in the dustbin. Bittu started clapping, and Mohanlal was in awe of what Milo did. Milo taught someone an unforgettable lesson-to keep the surroundings clean.

Days passed by, but Milo kept practicing what he learned from Rohan, Mona, and Sahil. He came to be known as the canine-vigilante in the slum area. Gradually, people started learning to keep their surroundings clean by putting waste in bins.

A few weeks later, Mohanlal was working at his thela, with Milo sitting beside him. While packing food for a customer using a newspaper, a dog's picture caught Mohanlal's attention. Mohanlal became curious and started reading. The dog in the picture looked very similar to Milo and also had a bandana around its neck. As Mohanlal read the whole section, he found that a family was looking for the dog. He also saw a phone number provided below the photo.

Mohanlal dialed the number and informed the family that he had found the dog they were looking for. He could sense the joy in Mona's voice over the phone. Mona thanked Mohanlal, choking in gratitude.

Milo became attentive, and his ears perked. He could hear the soft tone of Mona's voice through the high speaker volume of Mohanlal's phone. He started wagging his tail in excitement. Mohanlal bent down, held Milo's face in his palms, and said, "You are going home, friend".

Mohanlal closed his thela and started walking towards home, as he had informed Mona to meet them there. But, as soon as they reached home, they saw Bittu looking pale and lying on the ground. Sushila was not around. Mohanlal rushed towards Bittu and picked him up. He started rubbing his back and feet. He then ran inside the hut to get his medicines. He called Sushila for help. Sushila was in the neighborhood and rushed in with a few other nearby residents. Not knowing what was happening, Milo stood beside Bittu confused.

Suddenly, Milo heard someone's voice and was alerted. It had been long since he heard this voice, and he knew instantly who it was. Only one thing mattered to Milo now—the voice calling his name, getting louder and louder. He barked in utter excitement and bolted outside. His beautiful eyes sparkled with joy.

It was none other than Rohan calling out his name, again and again, his voice getting louder each time. Milo followed the voice and barked with his full strength.

Rohan, Mona, and Sahil saw Milo and ran towards him. They all reunited, and Milo could not contain his happiness. Rohan could not stop crying. Sahil and Mona tried to wipe their tears. They knelt on the road and hugged Milo whose tail would not stop wagging! Milo jumped in happiness while trying to lick Rohan's face. It looked like a joyous reunion to anyone watching them.

Everyone took some time to control their emotions. Suddenly, Milo realised that Bittu was unwell and started pulling Sahil's pants towards Mohanlal's house. Sahil could not understand what Milo was trying to convey but followed his lead. Soon, they could see that Milo had dragged them to a house that was crowded with people who looked distressed.

They all entered the house and saw a young boy of Rohan's age lying on the floor. The boy was Bittu, who was breathing heavily. His parents looked helpless. Sahil rushed to Mohanlal and enquired what was happening. Mohanlal explained Bittu's breathing problem to Sahil and Mona. Mona immediately came to action and offered help to take Bittu to the hospital.

The family along with Bittu and Mohanlal got in the car and drove to the hospital. Mohanlal was hopeful that Bittu would get help in time. Once they reached, the doctors took care of Bittu and gave him the required medicines.

While Bittu was resting, the doctor called everyone to his cabin and enquired further about Bittu's medical history. Mohanlal asked the doctor what was causing Bittu's breathing problem. "AIR POLLUTION", said the doctor. Curious Rohan asked the doctor what air pollution was. The doctor pulled up a chart that showed various activities around us that cause air pollution. He showed them various tiny particles that harm our lungs and make breathing difficult.

Rohan was curious to understand who caused the pollution. The doctor then explained to everyone that it is WE, HUMANS, who cause pollution and harm the environment. Rohan was surprised, and Mohanlal could not understand why only Bittu was impacted by air pollution.

The doctor responded, "There are many children, elderly people, and women who are severely impacted by air pollution". He continued, "People who work in various industries, drive vehicles, or work at construction sites also get impacted."

Rohan was still trying to understand how humans created air pollution. He was focusing on the chart and turned to Sahil. He enquired how cars are polluting the environment, as he always felt safe and healthy inside their car. Sahil explained to him how the fuel used in cars pollutes the air.

Meanwhile, Milo was also concentrating on various images on the chart, which showed smoke from vehicles, open fires, dust on road, and smoke from industries, among other things. He started relating these images to the moment when he was lost and was affected by smoke from auto-rickshaw, open fires near thelas, dust due to sweeping, smoke from chulhas, and waste burning; the list was endless.

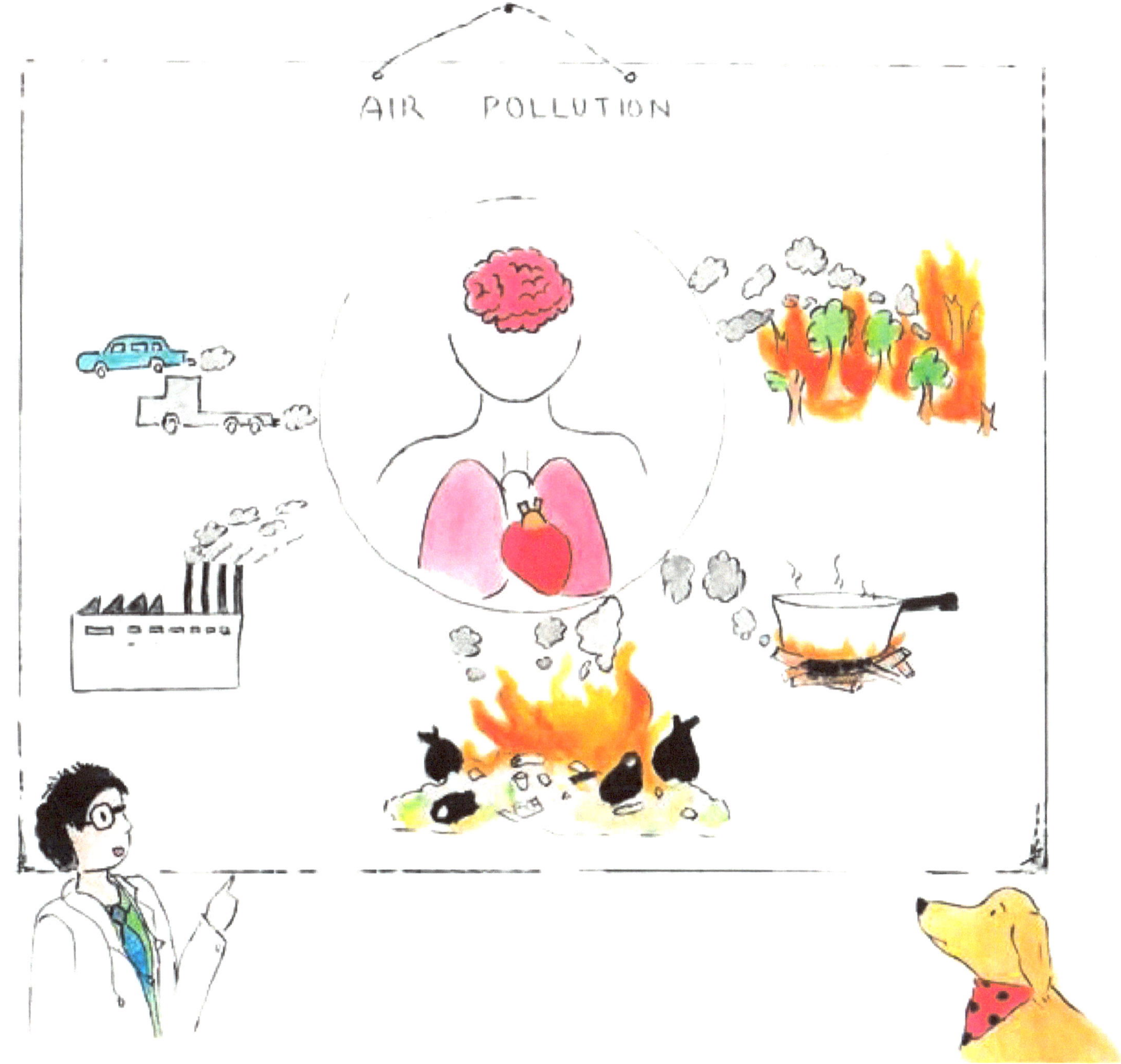

*Air pollution affects many human organs including the lungs, heart, and brain.

The family discussed with the doctor what could be the permanent 'Solution for Pollution' so that everyone could be safe and healthy. The doctor said, "Using an electric or gas stove for cooking, not burning waste, using electric vehicles, and using green technology in industries are some of the solutions.

However, for Mohanlal, arranging three meals for his family was a priority over air pollution. His financial condition was not good enough that he could buy an electric or gas stove. Disappointed with his situation, Mohanlal started thinking of other ways he could improve the air around him to help Bittu.

Meanwhile, Bittu gained consciousness and was feeling better. The family drove Bittu and Mohanlal to their home. Milo was not ready to leave Bittu. Seeing the affection and concern Milo had developed for Bittu, Sahil offered to help Mohanlal's family since they took care of Milo and helped them reunite with him. Mona and Sahil gave Mohanlal's family a cooking stove and gas cylinder, which would produce no smoke. Mohanlal could not thank him enough. Seeing everyone happy, Milo jumped with joy and showered his love on Bittu.

Mona and Sahil took a pledge that day to ensure cleaner air around them. They took the responsibility to educate adults and kids and create awareness in society on how to prevent air pollution.

A few months passed by. Whenever Mona would take Milo for evening walks, he would notice things around him. Once, he saw a car spewing black smoke while waiting at the signal. Milo remembered the doctor's chart and got angry. He started barking and pulling Mona towards the car. Mona could understand what Milo was indicating. She approached the traffic police and asked them to inquire about the pollution control certificate of the vehicle. It so happened that the vehicle was due for a pollution check for 2 months, and so, he was fined by the traffic police. Mona felt satisfied that they took a small yet important step toward clean air. She was proud of Milo and his presence of mind.

Milo started doing more to keep his surroundings clean. Not only would he now bark at people who did not use a dustbin but he also picked up litter himself to put it in the dustbin. He would also join Mona in her awareness programs. Milo and Rohan would assist Mona with some activities and help people understand how to segregate wastes and keep the air clean.

In this way, Milo's small misadventure led to bigger steps, improving the world he lived in!

Activity- Tick the correct answer/answers

1. What causes air pollution?

2. How can we reduce air pollution?

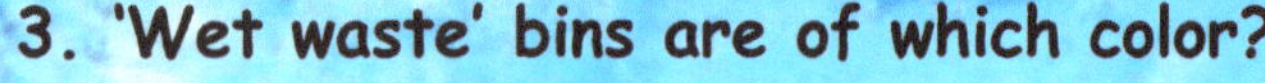

3. 'Wet waste' bins are of which color?

Milo is a cheerful dog leading an ordinary life, but one event changes his vision toward the environment. Will Milo understand the environmental challenges that humans, flora, and fauna face? Will Milo take the role of being an environment protector and realise his true purpose? Join Milo on his extraordinary journey and discover how he impacted humans around him through his witty behaviour and empathy.

Air pollution is a growing concern that is impacting men, women, children, and the elderly. Children are the victims of several health concerns due to air pollution. This book attempts to introduce air pollution to our young readers, with the hope to inspire them to become Clean Air Marshals like Milo in the fight for better air quality.

CSTEP acknowledges the support of Bloomberg Philanthropies for narrating this story and creating awareness on AIR POLLUTION.

www.ingramcontent.com/pod-product-compliance
Lightning Source LLC
LaVergne TN
LVHW071129160826
845679LV00005B/1221
* 9 7 9 8 8 9 0 2 6 7 4 7 4 *